Reconciliation
Services through the Church Year

Margrit Anna Banta

Homily Suggestions from Rev. Joseph A. Slattery

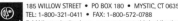

TWENTY-THIRD PUBLICATIONS
185 WILLOW STREET • PO BOX 180 • MYSTIC, CT 06355
TEL: 1-800-321-0411 • FAX: 1-800-572-0788
E-MAIL: ttpubs@aol.com • www.twentythirdpublications.com

The Scripture passages contained herein are from the *New Revised Standard Version of the Bible*, copyright © 1989, by the Division of Christian Education of the National Council of Churches in the U.S.A. All rights reserved.

Twenty-Third Publications
A Division of Bayard
185 Willow Street
P.O. Box 180
Mystic, CT 06355
(860) 536-2611 or (800) 321-0411
www.twentythirdpublications.com
ISBN:1-58595-313-X

Library of Congress Catalog Card Number: 2004100442
Printed in the U.S.A.

Contents

Introduction

In the gospel of Mark, Jesus tells us to "reform your lives and believe in the gospel" (Mk 1:15). Our liturgical celebrations of reconciliation prepare us to receive the sacrament. The hymns, prayers, Scripture readings, homily, and examination of conscience all move us toward repentance, reform, and a renewed relationship with God.

Reconciliation is one of the sacraments of healing and is known under several names. The *Catechism of the Catholic Church* mentions five: the sacrament of conversion, the sacrament of penance, the sacrament of confession, the sacrament of forgiveness, and the sacrament of reconciliation. The call to conversion is the first step in the process of returning to God. Confession of sins and penance lead to forgiveness, to reconciliation with the source of all being.

We have chosen the title *Reconciliation Services through the Church Year* to underscore the need we have to be reconciled with God and one another all year through. These services are grouped according to the liturgical year, though each can easily be adapted and used at other times. The services suggested for Ordinary Time, for example, can be adapted to Advent and Lent through use of appropriate seasonal songs. In each service, songs are suggested, but no specific recommendations are made since parishes vary widely in their use of liturgical music.

Suggestions for each service are contained in the Leader's Notes and are intended to enhance the service with visuals, activities, or ritual actions. These are optional suggestions and can be adapted to your own parish setting. If your parish is very large and confessors are few, you might want to ask the presider to give a penance before individual confessions so that penitents can leave after a period of quiet prayer, rather then wait for everyone to finish confessing. Conversely, should the celebrant wish to impart a final blessing, and the service does not provide for it, a sign of peace, an Our Father, a final blessing, and a closing song can always be added. Included with each service are Homily Suggestions by Father Joseph Slattery, intended to be just that, suggestions for the presider that make connections between the Scripture and the daily lives of participants.

May these services be a source of peace, healing, and forgiveness for you and your parishioners—all year through.

Let There Be Light

Leader's Notes

This service uses the images of light and darkness as metaphors for good and evil, as they are often used in Scripture.

To set the mood, the lights in church should be dimmed at the beginning of the service and turned up after the "Lord have mercy."

To further enhance the "light" theme, place seven large candles in a prominent place and after each response of the Examination of Conscience, have someone pre-appointed to light them. The ringing of a hand bell can further enhance this moment.

A final prayer and blessing are included in this service. However, if your congregation is large, it may be appropriate for the presider to give a penance before individual confessions. People can then leave quietly following absolution and some moments of quiet prayer.

Homily Suggestions

In the physical world, light and darkness are opposites. Darkness is the absence of light. When there is no light, it is dark, and, when light is present, darkness is absent. Light was part of God's creation in the beginning, as the first reading reminds us.

Light and darkness are commonplace experiences in our everyday world. The sun rises and dispels the darkness. The sun sets, and darkness sets in. We're not comfortable with darkness, because it can leave us blind and fearful. We're drawn towards light.

Light and darkness also have powerful symbolic meanings. For example, when Jesus says "I am the light of the world," we know immediately that he is speaking about more than physical light. Or, when during the Last Supper, Judas leaves the room and sets out to betray the Lord, John writes, "it was night," and we know that he is telling us something more than the time of day. Darkness and light have come to symbolize the good and evil in our everyday world; they have also come to symbolize the good and evil we experience within ourselves.

There's a difference here from physical light and darkness. In the physical world, light and darkness cannot co-exist together. But we are conscious of the fact that, within us, there is both light and darkness, and one element never succeeds entirely in conquering the other. We want to walk in the light, but sometimes the darkness overwhelms us. As St. Paul wrote to the Romans: "My inner self agrees with the law of God, but I see in my body's members another law at war with the law of my mind." Like Paul, we're all fragile disciples.

Light is a symbol of hope, and we have come here together today because the light is drawing us. We feel the pull of the light that is Jesus Christ, and we want to be children of the light. We know that we have been "enlightened," that is, brought into the light, by our baptism. But we are conscious, too, of the darkness that is in us—and sometimes the darkness seems to be more attractive than the light. So we approach this sacrament called a "second baptism" by the early Christians, to respond to the Lord's invitation in the gospel to come into the light. We want the light that symbolizes the Spirit's presence to shine more brightly within us, to strengthen us against the power of darkness and give us the courage to be faithful.

Let There Be Light

Opening Song

Opening Prayer

Presider	Let us pray. Eternal God, from the beginning of time we have yearned for closeness with you; it is our sins that have kept us from you. Today we come to ask forgiveness and to be enlightened by your Word, so that we can start again on the path of light that leads to you. We ask this in the name of Jesus, our Lord.
All	Amen.
Presider	Lord, we come as sinners, asking for pardon, and so we pray: Lord have mercy.
All	Lord have mercy.
Presider	Lord, you told us to forgive as we have been forgiven, and so we pray: Christ have mercy.
All	Christ have mercy
Presider	Lord, we seek your light, that we may again walk as children of light, and so we pray: Lord have mercy.
All	Lord have mercy.
Presider	May the Lord of mercy open our hearts and minds so that we may see more clearly how to love one another and then turn back to God in all that we do.
All	Amen.

First Reading: Genesis 1:1-5

In the beginning when God created the heavens and the earth, the earth was a formless void and darkness covered the face of the deep, while a wind from God swept over the face of the waters. Then God said, "Let there be light"; and there was light. And God saw that the light was good; and God separated the light from the darkness. God called the light Day, and the darkness Night. And there was evening and there was morning, the first day.

Responsorial Psalm (Psalm 27)

Reader One   Lord, you are my light and my salvation, whom should I fear?

All   Lord, you are my light and my salvation, whom should I fear?

Reader Two   Lord, you are my life's refuge, of whom should I be afraid?

All   Lord, you are my light and my salvation, whom should I fear?

Reader One   One thing I ask of you Lord, this I seek: to dwell in your house all the days of my life.

All   Lord, you are my light and my salvation, whom should I fear?

Reader Two   May I keep my gaze upon you and put my trust in you in the day of trouble.

All   Lord, you are my light and my salvation, whom should I fear?

Second Reading: Isaiah 42:5-7

Thus says God, the Lord, who created the heavens and stretched them out, who spread out the earth and what comes from it, who gives breath to the people upon it and spirit to those who walk in it: I am the Lord, I have called you in righteousness, I have taken you by the hand and kept you; I have given you as a covenant to the people, a light to the nations, to open the eyes that are blind, to bring out the prisoners from the dungeon, from the prison those who sit in darkness.

Gospel Acclamation

Alleluia. Alleluia. You are the light in the darkness. Shine your light upon us. Alleluia. Alleluia.

Gospel Reading: John 12:35-36a

Jesus said to them, "The light is with you for a little longer. Walk while you have the light, so that the darkness may not overtake you. If you walk in the darkness, you do not know where you are going. While you have the light, believe in the light, so that you may become children of light."

Homily

Meditation Song (or three minutes of silent meditation)

Examination of Conscience

Reader One   For the times we have walked in darkness and turned away from the light of your grace...

All   Lord, we ask for healing.

Light the first candle and/or ring the hand bells.

Reader Two   For the times we have withheld the light of goodness, patience, and forgiveness from our family members or friends...

All   Lord, we ask for healing.

Light the second candle and/or ring the hand bells.

Reader One   For the times we have given bad example in the workplace...

All   Lord, we ask for healing.

Light the third candle and/or ring the hand bells.

Reader Two   For neglecting to speak out against injustice on behalf of the poor and the voiceless...

All   Lord, we ask for healing.

Light the fourth candle and/or ring the hand bells.

Reader One   For choosing and valuing material goods when others' needs were greater than our own...

All   Lord, we ask for healing.

Light the fifth candle and/or ring the hand bells.

Reader Two   For the times we have lied about or passed judgment on others...

All   Lord, we ask for healing.

Light the sixth candle and/or ring the hand bells.

Presider   For the times we have hidden from the light when called to take a stand for peace, justice, and the common good...

All   Lord, we ask for healing.

Light the seventh candle and/or ring the hand bells.

Presider   As children of God, called into the light, let us pray together the Lord's Payer.

All   Our Father, who art in heaven...

Invitation to Confession

Final Prayer and Blessing

Presider   Merciful God, you have heard our prayers and freed us from our transgressions. In doing so, you have offered us your own gift of light; in thanksgiving, we now share a sign of peace with one another.

Exchange a sign of peace, for example: "The Light of Christ be with you."

Presider   Let us pray: May the Lord Jesus bless you and protect you, may he guide you and keep you always in his light.

All   Amen.

Presider   May the Lord Jesus help you to stay true to the promises you have made today and protect you from all harm, in the name of the Father and of the Son and of the Holy Spirit.

All   Amen.

Closing Song

Prepare the Way of the Lord

Leader's Notes

This service is based on a reading from the prophet Isaiah which is used during the Advent season. It challenges us to prepare ourselves for the coming of the Lord. While Isaiah speaks about a return from exile nearly 3000 years ago, his message is still fresh, for we, too, are in exile when we cut ourselves off from our Savior God.

In preparation for the service, write the following "actions," each on a separate (small) piece of paper (colored paper or parchment paper is nice, if available).

- Visit someone in a nursing home
- Pray a decade of the rosary
- Call someone who is housebound and offer your help
- Spend ten minutes at prayer
- Read a verse from Scripture and reflect on it
- Listen attentively to a coworker this week
- Make a contribution to a charity

- Practice patience at home with your family
- Perform an irksome task with a cheerful attitude
- Turn off the TV for an hour
- Make some small improvement in your neighborhood
- Contact someone from whom you are estranged

Roll these papers and tie them with a simple ribbon. Place them in a basket in a prominent place in the church. Following confession, invite each person to pick up one of the scrolls and do the suggested action.

Homily Suggestions

All of us have seen TV pictures of an important person arriving at some venue and being surrounded by a crowd of people; aides and bodyguards are on either side, while others run ahead to clear a path. We watch people being moved out of the way until a passage is opened up to let the person pass through.

This image of clearing a path ahead of someone is used twice in the readings we have just heard. In the first reading it refers to Yahweh's invitation to the Jewish exiles to set out across the desert and return to Jerusalem after fifty years of exile in Babylon. The prophet announces that God wants a pathway to be cleared for them through the desert. In the gospel reading, Mark uses the same language to describe the preaching task of John the Baptist in the Judean desert; he is preparing a way for the Lord, making a straight path before him. This work is being accomplished by proclaiming a baptism of repentance that would lead to the forgiveness of sins. Obviously, Mark is using the expression "prepare a way for the Lord" here as a metaphor. It is no longer meant to refer to clearing the way for the exiles in Babylon to travel a long journey through desert places. It refers instead to an inner journey, a spiritual journey that is also signified by the word "repentance."

We might ask ourselves: why does the gospel use the image of "clearing a path for the Lord" as a way of describing this journey? Because clearing a path involves getting rid of the obstacles that lie in the way. That task must be the foundation of our repentance. If we want to prepare a way for the Lord, we need to clear obstacles out of the way.

Some of the most basic obstacles that block our vision of the Lord are our own attitudes. Yet many people don't see that. They confess a particular action, but they never look beneath it to the sinful attitude that caused that action. It's like treating the symptom instead of the disease. For example, a person may take aspirin for a headache, but if that headache is caused by a brain tumor, it will continue until a more radical cure is applied. In the same way, I may confess to the sin of jealousy, but if I am ignoring the fact that I am always consumed with jealousy, I am not dealing with the real sin. Or, I may confess to having treated a co-worker badly, or to have spoken harshly to someone, but not be willing to confront the pride or anger that lay beneath my behavior.

So, as we approach this healing sacrament of forgiveness, we must confront the issue of destructive attitudes. Are we going to "prepare a way for the Lord" by just clipping the weeds that lie in the path, or are we prepared to tear them out by the roots? Isaiah promised God's blessings and peace to those who were willing to let go of their comfortable existence in Babylon and set out for the promised land. These blessings are meant for us too.

Prepare the Way of the Lord

Opening Song

Opening Prayer

Presider	Let us begin this time together with hearts and minds open: In the name of the Father and the Son and the Holy Spirit.
All	Amen.
Presider	The Lord of goodness and peace be with you.
All	And also with you.

Prayer for Forgiveness

Presider	Let us pray: Eternal Father, you sent your son to show us the way to eternal life. We want to follow this "way" ever more closely, and so we seek forgiveness for the times we have failed by straying from this path. Give us the courage to start anew and to follow Jesus more closely. We ask this in Jesus' name.
All	Amen.
Presider	Lord Jesus, you came to redeem a sinful people, and so we pray, Lord have mercy.
All	Lord have mercy.
Presider	Lord Jesus, you show us the way of life, and so we pray, Christ have mercy.
All	Christ have mercy.
Presider	Lord Jesus, you strengthen our faith, our hope and our love, so that we may follow you more closely, and so we pray, Lord have mercy.
All	Lord have mercy.
Presider	Hear us, O God, and have mercy on us. Make your healing presence known to us and forgive us our sins.
All	Amen.

First Reading: Isaiah 40:1-8

Comfort, O comfort my people, says your God. Speak tenderly to Jerusalem, and cry to her that she has served her term, that her penalty is paid, that she has received from the Lord's hand double for all her sins. A voice cries out in the wilderness, "Prepare the way of the Lord, make straight in the desert a highway for our God. Every valley shall be lifted up, and every mountain and hill be made low; the uneven ground shall become level, and the rough places a plain. Then the glory of the Lord shall be revealed, and all people shall see it together, for the mouth of the Lord has spoken." A voice says, "Cry out!" And I said, "What shall I cry?" All people are grass, their constancy is like the flower of the field. The grass withers, the flower fades, when the breath of the Lord blows upon it; surely the people are grass. The grass withers, the flower fades; but the word of our God will stand forever.

Responsorial Psalm (Psalm 25)

Reader One	O Lord, my God, to you I lift up my soul.
All	O Lord my God, to you I lift up my soul.
Reader Two	In you I trust; let me not be put to shame; let not my enemies exult over me.
All	O Lord my God, to you I lift up my soul.
Reader One	Your ways, O Lord, make known to me; teach me your paths.
All	O Lord my God, to you I lift up my soul.
Reader Two	Guide me in your truth and teach me, for you are God my savior, for you I wait all the day.
All	O Lord my God, to you I lift up my soul.
Reader One	Remember that your compassion, O Lord, and your kindness are from of old.
All	O Lord my God, to you I lift up my soul.
Reader Two	Good and upright is the Lord; thus he shows sinners the way. He guides the humble to justice, he teaches the humble his way.
All	O Lord my God, to you I lift up my soul.

Second Reading: 1 Thessalonians 1: 2-6

We always give thanks to God for all of you and mention you in our prayers, constantly remembering before our God and Father your work of faith and labor of love and steadfastness of hope in our Lord Jesus Christ. For we know, brothers and sisters beloved by God, that he has chosen you, because our message of the gospel came to you not in word only, but also in power and in the Holy Spirit and with full conviction; just as you know what kind of persons we proved to be among you for your sake. And you became imitators of us and of the Lord, for in spite of persecution you received the word with joy inspired by the Holy Spirit.

Gospel Acclamation

Alleluia. Alleluia. We are preparing a way for you in our hearts, O Lord. Alleluia. Alleluia.

Gospel Reading: Mark 1: 1-5

The beginning of the good news of Jesus Christ, the Son of God. As it is written in the prophet Isaiah, "See, I am sending my messenger ahead of you, who will prepare your way; the voice of one crying out in the wilderness: 'Prepare the way of the Lord, make his paths straight,'" John the baptizer appeared in the wilderness, proclaiming a baptism of repentance for the forgiveness of sins. And people from the whole Judean countryside and all the people of Jerusalem were going out to him, and were baptized by him in the river Jordan, confessing their sins.

Homily

Meditation Song (or three minutes of silent reflection)

Examination of Conscience

Reader One	For the times we have strayed from your path by ignoring the needs of others in our families and in our communities…
All	Lord, lead us back.
Reader Two	For the times we have strayed from your path by failing to accept responsibility for our anger, pride, jealousy, or greed…
All	Lord, lead us back.
Reader One	For the times we have strayed from your path by refusing to reconcile with those we have wronged…

All	Lord, lead us back.
Reader Two	For the times we have strayed from your path by failing to be peacemakers in our homes, parish, workplaces, and in our world…
All	Lord, lead us back.
Reader One	For the times we have strayed from your path by failing to heed the commandments you have given us…
All	Lord, lead us back.
Presider	Merciful and forgiving God, you are always ready to hear us and to lead us back. We come to you with contrite hearts. Give us your healing spirit and your forgiveness, that we might once again be firm in our resolve to follow you; we ask this in the name of Jesus, our Lord.
All	Amen.

Invitation to Confession

The Presider suggests a penance before individual confessions so people may leave quietly (following a time of reflection and prayer after confession). As each person leaves, he or she should pick up a scroll from the basket.

Follow the Star

Leader's Notes

Long ago, the Magi found the baby Jesus, the Messiah, by following a new star that had appeared in the heavens. As astrologers, they thought that a new star heralded an important event for all of humanity. In the season of Advent, we, too, look forward to an important event: the celebration of the coming of the messiah.

In this service, the star is the symbol of the search for Jesus, who is "the way, the truth, and the life."

For a visual display, suspend some large stars in the worship space, shiny stars cut out of metal sheeting material (or use stars sold in a craft store). If the service takes place shortly before Christmas, a tree can be put up in the worship area and each person can be asked to attach a star ornament following individual confessions. Or you might want to display an empty manger with the star near by and the three wise men (from your crèche) placed a distance away from the manger.

Homily Suggestions

The stars, the heavens, the sky, mountaintops; for thousands of years those things that draw human beings to look upward beyond themselves have had a sacred significance. They have come to symbolize the human longings for what is known as "transcendence," longings to break out of the limitations that bind us to this earth and all that is earthy, longings to leave behind us a legacy that will continue after we are gone, longings to come closer to God.

When God told Abraham to look up at the countless stars of the heavens and see there a symbol of his many descendants, he was being offered something that every person longed for in those days, a name and a memorial that would last through succeeding generations. When the Letter to the Hebrews praises all those people of faith from Abraham onward who fought the battles of faith and remained faithful to the end, it's talking about people who, like Abraham, looked up at the heavens and saw there something that called them to set out on a journey toward God. These people were motivated by a vision, born out of their experience of God, that inspired them to face the challenges and uncertainties of their lives with courage and confidence and a deep trust. Their story is recalled by the author of Hebrews in order to encourage us to follow in their footsteps.

Are we really following in their footsteps? Does the journey of those people of faith relate in any way to our own journey? Do we actually experience our faith-life as a journey that continues throughout our whole lives? When did that journey really begin for us? Can we look back to a time when we began to take seriously the promises made on our behalf at baptism, when we began to reach out for a personal experience of God? In what direction were we moved to go by that experience? How have we been following through since then on what happened to us at that time? Where are we now on our faith-journey? Are we conscious of moving forward or backward, or are we in a rut, without any sense of the Spirit's movement in our lives? Do we still experience that longing for transcendence, especially the longing for God, or are those words about struggle and faithfulness to the end that we just heard like a voice from the distant past that does not touch us now?

Perhaps we need to take advantage of this time of preparation for the sacrament of reconciliation to look back over the past year and ask ourselves if we really have been following the star, or if instead our hearts have been fixed on other things. What insight into the gospel has been guiding our lives, or have we too been affected by the kind of blindness that Jesus so often encountered? Are we bringing new life to people and situations that we're part of, or, on the contrary, are we draining life away from them?

It's so much easier to question others than to question ourselves. Some people might think that I have been asking too many questions. Yet, we need to question ourselves if we want to grow, and this sacrament is about a lot more than just wiping the slate clean, it's about looking up at the stars, about realizing that our journey is not over, about hearing the call to a fresh and more exciting journey to which the Lord will call us if and when we're ready.

Follow the Star

Opening Song

Opening Prayer

Presider	We begin our prayer together, in the name of the Father, and of the Son and of the Holy Spirit.
All	Amen.
Presider	The God of peace and forgiveness be with you.
All	And also with you.
Presider	Let us pray. Lord God, creator of the universe, you made the descendants of Abraham, our Father in faith, as numerous as the stars in the sky. A star led the three wise men to you. Lead us to you, too, for we long for your peace and forgiveness. We ask this in the name of Jesus your son, who lives forever and ever.
All	Amen.

Prayer for Forgiveness

Presider	With our hearts open to God, our father, Jesus our brother, and the Holy Spirit our inspiration, let us pray:
All	I confess to Almighty God, and to you, my brothers and sisters, that I have sinned through my own fault in my thoughts and my words, in what I have done, and in what I have failed to do; and I ask blessed Mary, ever Virgin, all the angels and saints, and you, my brothers and sisters to pray for me to the Lord, our God.

First Reading: Genesis 22:15-18

The angel of the Lord called to Abraham from heaven and said, "By myself I have sworn, says the Lord: Because you have done this, and have not withheld your son, your only son, I will indeed bless you, and I will make your offspring as numerous as the stars of heaven and as the sand that is on the seashore. And your offspring shall possess the gate of their enemies, and by your offspring shall all the nations of the earth gain blessing for themselves, because you have obeyed my voice."

Responsorial Psalm (Psalm 85)

Reader One   O Lord, show us your kindness and grant us your salvation.

All   O Lord, show us your kindness and grant us your salvation.

Reader Two   I will hear what you proclaim, O God, for you promise peace to your people, and to your faithful ones, and to those who put their hope in you.

All   O Lord, show us your kindness and grant us your salvation.

Reader One   Near indeed is your salvation to those who fear you, Glory dwelling in our land.

All   O Lord, show us your kindness and grant us your salvation.

Reader Two   Kindness and truth shall meet; justice and peace shall kiss. Truth shall spring out of the earth, and justice shall look down from heaven.

All   O Lord, show us your kindness and grant us your salvation.

Reader One   You yourself will give us benefits; our land shall yield its increase. Justice shall walk before you, and salvation along the way of your steps.

All   O Lord, show us your kindness and grant us your salvation.

Second Reading: Hebrews 11:8-14; 12:1-2

By faith Abraham obeyed when he was called to set out for a place that he was to receive as an inheritance; and he set out, not knowing where he was going. By faith he stayed for a time in the land he had been promised, as in a foreign land, living in tents, as did Isaac and Jacob, who were heirs with him of the same promise. For he looked forward to the city that has foundations, whose architect and builder is God. By faith he received power of procreation, even though he was too old—and Sarah herself was barren—because he considered him faithful who had promised. Therefore from one person, and this one as good as dead, descendants were born, "as many as the stars of heaven and as the innumerable grains of sand by the seashore." All of these died in faith without having received the promises, but from a distance they saw and greeted them. They confessed that they were strangers and foreigners on the earth, for people who speak in this way make it clear that they are seeking a homeland.

Therefore, since we are surrounded by so great a cloud of witnesses, let us also lay aside every weight and the sin that clings so closely, and let us run with perseverance the race that is set before us, looking to Jesus the pioneer and perfecter of our faith, who for the sake of the joy that was set before him endured the cross, disregarding its shame, and has taken his seat at the right hand of the throne of God.

Gospel Acclamation

Alleluia. Alleluia. We trust in your promise, O God, to lead us out of darkness into your great light. Alleluia. Alleluia.

Gospel: Matthew 2:1-12

In the time of King Herod, after Jesus was born in Bethlehem of Judea, wise men from the East came to Jerusalem, asking, "Where is the child who has been born king of the Jews? For we observed his star at its rising, and have come to pay him homage." When King Herod heard this, he was frightened, and all Jerusalem with him; and calling together all the chief priests and scribes of the people, he inquired of them where the Messiah was to be born. They told him, "In Bethlehem of Judea; for so it has been written by the prophet: 'And you, Bethlehem, in the land of Judah, are by no means least among the rulers of Judah; for from you shall come a ruler who is to shepherd my people Israel.'" Then Herod secretly called for the wise men and learned from them the exact time when the star had appeared. Then he sent them to Bethlehem, saying, "Go and search diligently for the child; and when you have found him, bring me word so that I may also go and pay him homage." When they had heard the king, they set out; and there, ahead of them, went the star that they had seen at its rising, until it stopped over the place where the child was. When they saw that the star had stopped, they were overwhelmed with joy. On entering the house, they saw the child with Mary his mother; and they knelt down and paid him homage. Then, opening their treasure chests, they offered him gifts of gold, frankincense, and myrrh. And having been warned in a dream not to return to Herod, they left for their own country by another road.

Homily

Meditation Song (or three minutes of silent reflection)

Examination of Conscience

Reader Two   Abraham tried to follow the commands of the Lord. For the times we have failed to live according to the laws and commandments of God, Lord have mercy…

All	Lord have mercy.
Reader One	Faith is confident assurance concerning what we hope for. For the times we have lost hope and faltered in our faith, Lord have mercy…
All	Lord have mercy.
Reader Two	Hope is a conviction that we will one day rest in you, O God. For the times we have doubted and failed to trust, Lord have mercy…
All	Lord have mercy.
Reader One	The magi remained faithful and followed the star. For the times we have followed our own interests and ignored the needs of others, Lord have mercy…
All	Lord have mercy.
Reader Two	Sarah believed that God would bless her. For the times we have looked for success and recognition rather than for inner growth, Lord have mercy…
All	Lord have mercy.

Invitation to Confession

Final Prayer and Blessing

Presider	Lord, we thank you for your healing presence here today. With your grace, we will continue to walk as children of the light. With this as our intention, we now offer a sign of peace to one another.

Exchange a sign of peace, for example: "May Christ's peace light your way."

Presider	May the blessings of the Father, the Son, and the Holy Spirit be upon you now and forever.
All	Amen.
Presider	Go forth and live in the peace of Christ.
All	Amen.

Closing Song

Create in Me a New Heart

Leader's Notes

Conversion calls for a change of heart, a change that brings us ever closer to the way of the gospel. As a symbol of this change, place a large open heart in your worship space. This symbol can be constructed from a cardboard box. Cut the heart out of the top of the box. For a shadow box effect, drape a large cloth over the box. Push the center of the cloth to the inside, so that it becomes a liner and drape the ends over the sides, tucking them under the box. A red cloth would provide a dramatic visual effect. Have available rough-edged small stones for each person. Such stones are available in large bags from most garden centers. (Greeters can hand these out as people enter the church.)

Homily Suggestions

There is no way to learn a new language without working through the fundamentals of that language. We may learn the correct pronunciation of some phrases, and what to say in certain situations, but, if we're not familiar with the basic grammar, we won't make much progress.

It's somewhat the same with the gospel. There's a certain veneer of Christianity in local culture that may sometimes pass for the real thing. Membership in a recognized church, attendance at prayer meetings, contributions to popular causes, and slogans with Christian themes provide the trappings of discipleship and may seem to communicate, to ourselves and others, that we're disciples of Jesus Christ. But we need to return over and over again to the fundamentals, and ask ourselves whether or not we have actually mastered the basics.

That's the issue Jesus addresses in the gospel we have just heard, where a scribe asks him what the most important commandment of the Law is. He responds by quoting from the well-known words of Deuteronomy (chapter six), words that were part of the daily prayer of devout Jews, and adding a second commandment from the Book of Leviticus, "you shall love your neighbor as yourself."

Let's reflect on the words of Deuteronomy first of all: "Hear, O Israel, the Lord our God is Lord alone!" We might respond to the challenge of this command by saying, "Of course we worship one God; we're not idol-worshippers!" But is this actually the case? Have we made our own the exhortation to love God with all our heart, all our soul, all our mind, and all our strength? The challenge of these words confronts us with a key question: where are the longings of our heart? Is it not true that the daily longings of our heart are much more likely to be focused anywhere but on God, that such things as money, cars, electronic gadgets, clothes, improving our personal appearance, getting ahead of others, keeping up with the Joneses, are much more likely to occupy our thoughts and desires than the issue of how to express our love for God? In other words, our hearts are often focused on what will bring satisfaction and pleasure to ourselves, what will make us feel good. In the ongoing conflict between gospel and culture, we seem to have taken sides, and many of our decisions find us in conflict with the spirit of the gospel. We may not be idol-worshippers in the ancient sense, but often it is only because new idols have replaced the old.

Jesus also proposed a second commandment: "you shall love your neighbor as yourself." Prejudice will probably always exist in the human heart, as well as the resulting discrimination against people who are in some way different. Let's examine ourselves for a moment with regard to one particular root of prejudice: nationalism. God sees no national boundaries. All peoples of the earth are God's children, and no one person or nation has a greater claim on God's blessings than another. Nationalism can blind us to that basic truth of the gospel. It can convey the illusion that, as they say, "God is on our side," that we can look around at the good things we see in our own country and feel superior to those who are on the other side of our national boundaries. Nothing could be farther from the truth; our many blessings should be a source of responsibility rather than of pride. "Love your neighbor as yourself."

Reflecting on the fundamentals of the gospel should be a reminder that we haven't taken these fundamentals seriously enough. We need to hear the call to conversion once again. We need a new heart.

Create in Me a New Heart

Opening Song

Opening Prayer

Presider	We begin our prayer together in the name of the Father, and of the Son, and of the Holy Spirit.
All	Amen.
Presider	May the peace and the mercy of God be with you.
All	And also with you.
Presider	Let us pray: Gracious God, we come to you burdened by sin and with heartfelt sorrow, seeking your forgiveness. Heal us from all that weighs us down: our transgressions, our fears, and our anxieties. Reach out to us and cleanse our hearts. We ask this through our Lord Jesus Christ, your Son, who lives and reigns with you and the Holy Spirit, forever and ever.
All	Amen.

Prayer for Forgiveness

Reader One	Lord, we acknowledge our sinfulness against you and against one another, Lord, have mercy.
All	Lord have mercy.
Reader Two	Christ, teach us to forgive, as we have been forgiven. Christ, have mercy.
All	Christ, have mercy.
Reader One	Lord, we look to you for help; you are our healer and our guide, Lord have mercy.
All	Lord have mercy.
Presider	Father, you know our human weakness and how we have hardened our hearts. Help us to look into our hearts, to see ourselves more clearly, so that we can learn to love you and our neighbor more sincerely.
All	Amen.

First Reading: Ezekiel 36:24-28, 31-32

I will take you from the nations, and gather you from all the countries, and bring you into your own land. I will sprinkle clean water upon you, and you shall be clean from all your uncleannesses, and from all your idols I will cleanse you. A new heart I will give you, and a new spirit I will put within you; and I will remove from your body the heart of stone and give you a heart of flesh. I will put my spirit within you, and make you follow my statutes and be careful to observe my ordinances. Then you shall live in the land that I gave to your ancestors; and you shall be my people, and I will be your God.

Then you shall remember your evil ways, and your dealings that were not good; and you shall loathe yourselves for your iniquities and your abominable deeds. It is not for your sake that I will act, says the Lord God; let that be known to you. Be ashamed and dismayed for your ways, O house of Israel.

Responsorial Psalm (Psalm 51)

Reader One   Create in me a clean heart, O God, and put a new spirit within me.

All   Create in me a clean heart, O God.

Reader Two   Do not cast me away from your presence, and do not take your Holy Spirit from me.

All   Create in me a clean heart, O God.

Reader One   Restore me to the joy of your salvation, and sustain in me a willing spirit.

All   Create in me a clean heart, O God.

Reader Two   Then I will teach transgressors your ways, and sinners will return to you.

All   Create in me a clean heart, O God.

Second Reading: 1 Timothy 1:12-17

I am grateful to Christ Jesus our Lord, who has strengthened me, because he judged me faithful and appointed me to his service, even though I was formerly a blasphemer, a persecutor, and a man of violence. But I received mercy because I had acted ignorantly in unbelief, and the grace of our Lord overflowed for me with the faith and love that are in Christ Jesus. The saying is sure and worthy of full acceptance, that Christ Jesus came into the world to save sinners —of whom I am the foremost. But for that very reason I received mercy, so that in me, as the foremost, Jesus Christ might display the utmost patience, making me an example to those who would come to believe in him for eternal life. To the King of the ages, immortal, invisible, the only God, be honor and glory forever and ever. Amen.

Gospel Acclamation

Praise be to you, O Word of God, Lord Jesus Christ. You have seen our sins and you know our weaknesses. Yet you continue to love us. Praise be to you, O Word of God, Lord Jesus Christ.

Gospel: Mark 12:28-31

One of the scribes came near and asked Jesus, "Which commandment is the first of all?" Jesus answered, "The first is, 'Hear, O Israel: the Lord our God, the Lord is one; you shall love the Lord your God with all your heart, and with all your soul, and with all your mind, and with all your strength.' The second is this, 'You shall love your neighbor as yourself.' There is no other commandment greater than these."

Homily

Meditation Song (or three minutes of silent reflection)

Examination of Conscience

Reader Two	The prophet Ezekiel reminds us of the importance of a change of attitude. Are we willing to give up long-held grudges and prejudices?
All	Lord, change our hearts.
Reader One	Ezekiel reminds us that we need to change our conduct as well. Are we able to control our anger and love others unselfishly?
All	Lord, change our hearts.
Reader Two	When we gather as church, do we respect the aged, the children, and the disabled?
All	Lord, change our hearts.
Reader One	St. Paul writes about the importance of a sincere faith, admitting his own doubts and his arrogance. Can we admit our shortcomings and ask God for guidance?
All	Lord, change our hearts.

Reader Two	Jesus reminds us of the importance of the commandment to love God with all our heart, all our mind, and all our strength. Do we set aside time to pray and meditate, or do we allow the business of life and the lure of possessions to take over our time?
All	Lord, change our hearts.
Reader One	Jesus reminds us that we should love our neighbor as ourselves. Do we show love for all our neighbors, our co-workers, our relatives? Do we show love for ourselves by giving up unhealthy habits and by treating our bodies with care?
All	Lord, change our hearts.
Reader Two	Do we respect our neighbors, regardless of their ethnicity or station in life? Are we concerned about the homeless, prisoners, foreigners—all our brothers and sisters and neighbors?
All	Lord, change our hearts.
Presider	Forgiving God, take away our stony hearts and give us hearts ready to love. Give us your grace and your spirit so that we may experience the many blessings you have promised.
All	Amen.
Presider	Confident that the Lord hears our request, let us now pray as Jesus taught us:
All	Our Father, who art in heaven…

Invitation to Confession

Ask participants to carry their stones when they come forward to confess. After they receive absolution they should place the stones inside the heart—a sign that forgiveness and love change our hearts. Invite them, too, to spend quiet time in prayer and thanksgiving before leaving the church.

Now Is the Time of Salvation

Leader's Notes

In this lenten service, incense is a key component. The rising smoke is a symbol of our prayers rising up to God. (A hymn based on Psalm 141 would be an appropriate opening song.)

Additional censers can be constructed from large pottery saucers, available at garden centers. Fill these partially with sand and place a few charcoal rounds in the middle. Light these shortly before the service starts and have the incense nearby for the blessing. Several people from the congregation can be appointed to bring the censers to the priest for the blessing.

(Caution: Occasionally people are allergic to the smell of incense. Is there a place in your worship space a distance from the censers that could be designated for these people?)

Homily Suggestions

Most of us, as we go through life, develop our own ways of dealing with day-to-day problems. For example, we try to avoid difficult people or situations; or, if we have to be in the company of people who say things we don't like to hear, we "turn them off." In other words, we don't listen to them, even though we might pretend that we do.

Something similar seems to have happened with regard to the more challenging parts of the gospel. While we never get tired of hearing the beautiful parables and miracle stories, such as the prodigal son or the multiplication of the loaves and fishes, there are certain things that people don't really seem to hear, or, if they do, they seem to believe that they apply to others and not to themselves.

An example of this is the teachings of Jesus found in the sermon on the Mount. We have trained ourselves over the years to tune out sounds or words that don't appeal to us, or that don't seem to make much sense to us. So we can look quite devout and attentive as Jesus' sermon is once again proclaimed in church—but not actually attend to a word of it.

Some people might say, "The Ten Commandments are good enough for me." However, the commandments were a basic law for primitive people of three thousand years ago. Jesus went a long way beyond them. In fact, he even changed and re-worked some of them. So, even though we might be able to say truthfully, "I haven't killed anyone, or committed adultery, or worshipped idols, or given false witness against my neighbor," that doesn't necessarily qualify us to be called disciples of Jesus Christ. If we really want that name, we will, sooner or later, have to come to terms with the Sermon on the Mount.

Certainly, its message doesn't sound appealing: Jesus says, "Blessed are you poor," but we don't want to live a simple life; we'd like to win the lottery! "Blessed are you who are hungry," but our problem is more often avoiding overweight from eating too much. "Blessed are you who are weeping," but we want to stay away from sad people and have a good time. "Blessed are you when people hate you." On the contrary, we want everyone to like us. "When someone slaps you on one cheek, turn and offer the other." Is it possible that Jesus can be serious? Our culture tells us to get even when someone wrongs us.

As we listen once again to these words of the Lord, there can be a real sense of distance. It's like listening to someone speaking a foreign language; we hear the words but the meaning does not penetrate our hearts. It's a counter-cultural message that undermines how our culture tells us we should actually live.

A celebration of the sacrament of reconciliation is a good time to think about this. Too often, when we come to confess our sins, we tend to confine ourselves to commandments or laws of the church that we have broken. We need to look at the larger picture too, our lifestyle, the values we take for granted, our ambitions, our goals for ourselves, the things we put our greatest efforts into achieving. When we try to do this, the words of the Sermon on the Mount will take on new meaning for us.

Now Is the Time of Salvation

Opening Song

Opening Prayer

Presider	As we begin our prayer, let us give thanks for this time to gather in the presence of the Father, the Son, and the Holy Spirit.
All	Amen.
Presider	To prepare ourselves for this celebration, let us call to mind our transgressions.
Silent pause	
Presider	Lord, we have sinned against you; Lord have mercy.
All	Lord have mercy.
Presider	Lord, show us your mercy and love,
All	and grant us your salvation.
Presider	May the Lord be attentive to us and open our hearts, so that we may see the wrong we have done and be ready to seek forgiveness. We ask this in the name of Jesus Christ, our Lord,
All	Amen.

Invite those assigned to bring the censer or censers forward so the incense can be placed in them.

Prayer of Blessing Over the Incense

Presider	Lord our God, bless this incense as it burns here before us. May its smoke be a symbol of our prayers rising up to you; may its odor be a symbol of your healing power. As the coals turn to ashes, may our lives be changed; may we turn again to you in this time of salvation. We ask this through Christ, Our Lord.
All	Amen.

The presider incenses the people.

First Reading: 2 Corinthians 5:20-21, 6:1-2

We are ambassadors for Christ, since God is making his appeal through us; we entreat you on behalf of Christ, be reconciled to God. For our sake he made him to be sin who knew no sin, so that in him we might become the righteousness of God.

As we work together with him, we urge you also not to accept the grace of God in vain. For he says, "At an acceptable time I have listened to you, and on a day of salvation I have helped you." See, now is the acceptable time; see, now is the day of salvation!

Responsorial Psalm (Psalm 91)

All	Lord, you are our refuge and our strength.
Reader One	You who dwell in the shelter of the Most High, who abide in the shadow of the Almighty, say to the Lord, "my refuge and my fortress, my God, in whom I trust."
All	Lord, you are our refuge and our strength.
Reader Two	You, O God, rescue us from the snare of the fowler; with your pinions you cover us. Under your wings we take refuge; we will not fear the terror of the night.
All	Lord, you are our refuge and our strength.
Reader One	Because we have you for our refuge, we have made the most high our stronghold. No evil shall befall us; nor shall affliction come near us.
All	Lord, you are our refuge and our strength.
Reader Two	For to your angels you have given command about us, that they guard us in all our ways. Upon their hands they shall bear us up, lest we dash a foot against a stone.
All	Lord, you are our refuge and our strength.

Gospel Reading: Luke 6:17-38

Jesus came down with them and stood on a level place, with a great crowd of his disciples and a great multitude of people from all Judea, Jerusalem, and the coast of Tyre and Sidon. They had come to hear him and to be healed of their diseases; and those who were troubled with unclean spirits were cured. And all in the crowd were trying to touch him, for power came out from him and healed all of them. Then he looked up at his disciples and said: "Blessed are you who are poor, for yours is the kingdom of God. Blessed are you who are hungry now, for you will be filled. Blessed are you who weep now, for you will laugh. Blessed are you when people hate you, and when they exclude you, revile you, and defame you on account of the Son of Man. Rejoice in that day and leap for joy, for surely your reward is great in heaven; for that is what their ancestors did to the prophets. But woe to you who are rich, for you have received your consolation. Woe to you who are full now, for you will be hungry. Woe to you who are laughing now, for you will mourn and weep. Woe to you when all speak well of you, for that is what their ancestors did to the false prophets. But I say to you that listen, Love your enemies, do good to those who hate you, bless those who curse you, pray for those who abuse you. If anyone strikes you on the cheek, offer the other also; and from anyone who takes away your coat do not withhold even your shirt. Give to everyone who begs from you; and if anyone takes away your goods, do not ask for them again. Do to others as you would have them do to you. If you love those who love you, what credit is that to you? For even sinners love those who love them. If you do good to those who do good to you, what credit is that to you? For even sinners do the same. If you lend to those from whom you hope to receive, what credit is that to you? Even sinners lend to sinners, to receive as much again. But love your enemies, do good, and lend, expecting nothing in return. Your reward will be great, and you will be children of the Most High; for he is kind to the ungrateful and the wicked. Be merciful, just as your Father is merciful. Do not judge, and you will not be judged; do not condemn, and you will not be condemned. Forgive, and you will be forgiven; give, and it will be given to you. A good measure, pressed down, shaken together, running over, will be put into your lap; for the measure you give will be the measure you get back."

Homily

Meditation Song (or three minutes of silent reflection)

Examination of Conscience

Reader One	Blessed are you who are poor.
Reader Two	Have I reached out to the poor; have I shown respect for the homeless; have I tried to help? Have I tried to live simply; have I refused to waste resources that could benefit others?
All	Lord, to you we lift up our hearts.
Reader One	Blessed are you who are now hungry.

Reader Two	Have I tried to alleviate hunger; have I contributed to food collections? Have I been so concerned about my own needs that I neglected the needs of others? Have I remembered to be thankful for all the good things I have received?
All	Lord, to you we lift up our hearts.
Reader One	Blessed are you who are now weeping.
Reader Two	Have I tried to console someone who is sad? Have I shown compassion to someone who is needy? Have I tried to see the other side of an argument? Have I been a good listener?
All	Lord, to you we lift up our hearts.
Reader One	Love your enemies, do good to those who hate you.
Reader Two	Have I tried to set aside my prejudices and listen with an open mind? Have I been the first to offer forgiveness? Have I refused to seek revenge? Have I prayed for those who hate me?
All	Lord, to you we lift up our hearts.
Presider	Gracious God, ever loving and forgiving, we turn to you now for help. When we were still in sin, you redeemed us. Hear us now at this our time of salvation.
All	Amen.

Invitation to Confession

Final Prayer and Blessing

Presider	As a sign that we have been forgiven, let us raise our hands and recite together the prayer Jesus taught us:
All	Our Father, who art in heaven…
Presider	The Lord has freed us from our sins so that we can once more love and serve one another. May God now bless us: In the name of the Father and of the Son and of the Holy Spirit.
All	Amen.

Closing Song

I Am the Good Shepherd

Leader's Notes

This service uses the well-known and comforting image of the good shepherd who seeks out the one sheep that is lost. The good shepherd celebrates the return of the lost one, even calling together his friends to share his joy.

On a raised platform, arrange a display of a shepherd and several sheep (from your Christmas crèche). Cover the platform with straw and have a container of straw nearby. Each person can add a straw to the display after receiving the sacrament.

Homily Suggestions

In traditional cultures, customary ways of doing things can be handed down for thousands of years. An example of this can be seen even today among the shepherds of the Holy Land. From time immemorial, a shepherd travels with the flock from one location to another as the seasons change in order to find pasture and water. The shepherd also leads them to shelter in bad weather and protects them from robbers and wild animals. When a shepherd settles down with his sheep for the night, he first of all makes a circle of rocks and then gathers the sheep together and leads them inside the circle. Once they are inside, he lays down across the entrance.

Shepherds establish a remarkable relationship with their flocks; the sheep come to recognize their shepherd's voice and distinguish it from others, and they learn to obey commands given by voice. A shepherd might confidently leave the sheep to go in search of a stray, knowing that they will remain together until he returns. It's this ancient practice among pastoral cultures of leading, guarding, and protecting the sheep that has given rise to the many Scripture stories and parables about sheep and shepherds.

However, this image of shepherd and sheep is not one with which our Western culture (that values independence and self-reliance), is totally comfortable. We tend to be critical of people who, as they say, "go along with the herd." The image of a shepherd leading obedient, docile sheep to pasture is one that has been used in the church over many generations. But it doesn't seem to fit very well with the concept of shared responsibility or lay ministry and leadership in the church of today.

Something important to bear in mind is that passivity and unquestioned acceptance of authority were never what the biblical images of sheep and shepherd were meant to express. The image of "shepherd" was applied to God and to many levels of leadership in Israel from the king on down. Its use had to do primarily with relationships. It was meant to express a caring, healing, loving, protective service that was wholly dedicated to the well-being of the people, as a good shepherd's would have been for the sheep.

What we must take from the image of the Lord as our shepherd, then, is a picture of who Jesus is and how much he cares for us and protects us. It's an image of the shepherd who has laid down his life for us. As we approach the sacrament of reconciliation this is important to bear in mind, because this is a sacrament that expresses in a powerful way the Lord's caring, healing, and forgiving love for each one of us. It is the Lord putting his protective arms around us as the shepherd encircles his flock with protective rocks. It is the Lord's invitation to us to rest with him and find green pastures—to put aside our fears and experience his peace.

I Am the Good Shepherd

Opening Song

Opening Prayer

Presider	As the good shepherd goes searching for the sheep that are lost, so today we ask you, Christ Jesus, to forgive us our sins and welcome us back. We ask this in the name of the Father and of the Son and of the Holy Spirit.
All	Amen.
Presider	May the Lord's peace be with you,
All	And also with you.
Presider	Let us pray: Ever living God, you are the good shepherd who guides us and gathers us together. When we stray, you do not abandon us, but instead you seek us out and call us back to the fold. Hear our call and seek us once again. Give us the comfort of your presence, and the strength to follow you always. We ask this in Jesus' name.
All	Amen.
Presider	Lord have mercy.
All	Lord have mercy.
Presider	Christ have mercy.
All	Christ have mercy.
Presider	Lord have mercy.
All	Lord have mercy.

First Reading: Ezekiel 34:11-16

For thus says the Lord God: I myself will search for my sheep, and will seek them out. As shepherds seek out their flocks when they are among their scattered sheep, so I will seek out my sheep. I will rescue them from all the places to which they have been scattered on a day of clouds and thick darkness. I will bring them out from the peoples and gather them from the countries, and will bring them into their own land; and I will feed them on the mountains of Israel, by the watercourses, and in all the inhabited parts of the land. I will feed them with good pasture, and the mountain heights of Israel shall be their pasture; there they shall lie down in good grazing land, and they shall feed on rich pasture on the mountains of Israel. I myself will be the shepherd of my sheep, and I will make them lie down, says the Lord God. I will seek the lost, and I will bring back the strayed, and I will bind up the injured, and I will strengthen the weak, but the fat and the strong I will destroy. I will feed them with justice.

Responsorial Psalm (Psalm 23)

Reader One	You are my shepherd, Lord, I shall not want.
All	You are my shepherd, Lord, I shall not want.
Left Side	In verdant pastures you give me repose; beside restful waters you lead me; you refresh my soul.
All	You are my shepherd, Lord, I shall not want.
Right Side	You guide me in right paths for your name's sake.
Reader Two	Even though I walk in the dark valley, I fear no evil; for you are at my side.
All	You are my shepherd, Lord, I shall not want.
Left Side	You spread the table before me in the sight of my foes; you anoint my head with oil; my cup overflows.
All	You are my shepherd, Lord, I shall not want.
Right Side	Only goodness and kindness follow me all the days of my Life; and I shall dwell in the house of the Lord for years to come.
All	You are my shepherd, Lord, I shall not want.

Gospel Acclamation

Praise be to you, O Word of God, Lord Jesus Christ. You watch over us always, guiding us, blessing us. Praise be to you, O Word of God, Lord Jesus Christ.

Gospel Reading: Luke 15:1-7

Now all the tax collectors and sinners were coming near to listen to him. And the Pharisees and the scribes were grumbling and saying, "This fellow welcomes sinners and eats with them." So he told them this parable: "Which one of you, having a hundred sheep and losing one of them, does not leave the ninety-nine in the wilderness and go after the one that is lost until he finds it? When he has found it, he lays it on his shoulders and rejoices. And when he comes home, he calls together his friends and neighbors, saying to them, 'Rejoice with me, for I have found my sheep that was lost.' Just so, I tell you, there will be more joy in heaven over one sinner who repents than over ninety-nine righteous persons who need no repentance."

Homily

Meditation Song (or three minutes of silent reflection)

Examination of Conscience

Reader One	For the times we have forgotten to follow Jesus, the Good Shepherd…
All	Forgive us, O God.
Reader Two	For the times we have caused others to stray because of poor example…
All	Forgive us, O God.
Reader One	For the times we have ignored the needs of the poor, the hungry, the sick, and all of Jesus' least ones…
All	Forgive us, O God.
Reader Two	For all our sins and faults…
All	Forgive us, O God.

Prayer of Contrition

Presider	Let us recognize and acknowledge our sins before God and one another with a prayer of contrition, asking for forgiveness and reconciliation.
All	I confess to almighty God, and to you my brothers and sisters, that I have sinned through my own fault, in my thoughts and in my words, in what I have done and in what I have failed to do; and I ask blessed Mary ever Virgin, all the angels and saints, and you my brothers and sisters, to pray for me to the Lord our God.
Presider	May Jesus the good shepherd hear us, have mercy on us, forgive us our sins, and lead us safely home.
All	Amen.

Invitation to Confession

Invite participants (after they have received forgiveness) to add a straw to the shepherd display as a sign of their trust in Jesus, the Good Shepherd.

Final Prayer and Dismissal

Presider   Jesus our brother; in your unending love you call us to yourself again and again. We have been healed by your shepherd's care. Help us to carry your healing love to all we meet. Keep us together in harmony, unity, and steadfast faith, hope, and love.

All   Amen.

Presider   Let us now share a sign of peace with one another.

Exchange a sign of peace, for example: "The peace of Jesus our shepherd be with you."

Final Blessing

Presider   May you carry the blessings of the Lord to all you meet: In the name of the Father and of the Son and of the Holy Spirit.

All   Amen.

Closing Song

Why Have You Forsaken Me?

Leader's Notes

This service is based on a modified way of the cross drawn from gospel accounts of Jesus' passion and death. If your parish has a teen drama group, you might want to invite them to present a silent tableau for each station. Such a dramatic presentation makes the events present to participants in a powerful way.

Another option is to place a large cross in the worship area. As people enter the church give each a small card with the words of the "Stabat Mater" on it. These will be used as a response to each station. The words are: "At the cross her station keeping, stood the mournful mother weeping, close to Jesus to the last." After their individual confessions, invite participants to come forward to touch and/or kiss the cross.

Homily Suggestions

All of us live with pain of one kind or another, from the pain of a headache to the pain of a lost ideal. At times the pain is as small as a pin-prick, at other times it seems to be as great as the ocean. We run away from the pain; we get busy so we can distract ourselves from it; we endure it; we search for ways to accept it. We look for the power to embrace what we fear and to find the strength for acceptance. As we do that, we are seeking to learn the spirituality of the Cross, to enter into something that is full of mystery.

Sometimes what we are called upon to endure is too much for us. We may see dimly what the response should be, but we find ourselves unable to make it. We are suffering from a weariness of soul that holds us back. We find ourselves even tempted to give up. We may be tired of trying to do what seems impossible, trying to change what does not want to change.

A little criticism makes us angry, a little rejection makes us depressed. A little praise raises our spirits, and a little success excites us. It can take very little to raise us up or cast us down. Often we are like small boats on the ocean, completely at the mercy of the waves. All the time and energy we put into keeping some kind of balance and preventing ourselves from being tipped over, is a sign that we haven't really learned the spirituality of the cross.

And yet, the crosses of the moment, the crosses of the years, continue to touch us, to insist that we pay attention to our pain and brokenness. We keep coming up against the mystery of the cross, looking for the courage to live our faith, to respond to the gospel call, to make sense of the crucifixion.

But our lives are part of a greater reality. We live in a new world that is continually being born. We hear the cries of those who are struggling to survive, but we trust at the same time that there will be light for another day, strength for another journey, laughter and hope. We look at the cross, we hear the invitation to be lifted up so we can begin to see with the same vision that Jesus had. Can we discover new life when we find ourselves stripped of our hopes and security? Is it really true that power comes from embracing the wood of suffering and contradiction? The mystery and spirituality of the cross plunges us into a profound awareness of our own poverty, the poverty of emptiness, powerlessness, sinfulness, physical weakness, limitation, failure, and betrayal.

The spirituality of the cross includes our belief that in Jesus death has lost its sting. We believe that even though we may suffer pain, betrayal, and rejection, we can, through the saving love of Jesus, keep coming back to life, keep getting up when we appear to be overwhelmed, keep growing into healing and wholeness. Through our acceptance of our suffering we enter into our own inner depths and we find compassion. Out of this struggle we learn to put aside judgment and harshness. Daily we are called to go back in memory to the cross, to keep facing our fears and failure. The cross is not just "out there," it's in here, in my treatment of myself, in my disappointments, weakness, and sinfulness. In the cross is healing; in the cross is peace; in the cross is forgiveness and redemption.

Why Have You Forsaken Me?

Opening Song

Opening Prayer

Presider   As we contemplate the sufferings of Jesus during his final hours on earth, we begin in the name of the Father and of the Son and of the Holy Spirit.

All   Amen.

Presider   Let us pray. Gracious Lord Jesus, in all your words and deeds, in all your pain and suffering, you thought of us and our sins. Following the way of your passion and death, we now unite ourselves with you. Teach us to be compassionate, persevering, and forgiving. We ask this in your holy name.

All   Amen.

The agony in the garden

Reader One   Jesus went with his disciples to a place called Gethsemane. He said to them: "Stay here while I go over there and pray." He took along Peter and the two sons of Zebedee and soon Jesus began to experience sorrow and distress. He said to them: "My heart is nearly broken with sorrow. Remain here and stay awake with me." He advanced a little and fell prostrate in prayer. "My father, if it is possible, let this cup pass me by. Still, let it be as you would have it" (Matthew 26:36–42).

Reader Two   Jesus, you experienced great sorrow as your time of agony approached, yet in prayer you were able to offer yourself completely to God. Teach us to see the wisdom of the cross in our lives and to pray with heartfelt contrition. Forgive us for the times we have failed and sought only our own will.

Response: Stabat Mater

All   At the cross her station keeping
Stood the mournful Mother, weeping.
Close to Jesus to the last.

Jesus is condemned

Reader One At daybreak the chief priests and elders took formal action against Jesus to put him to death. They bound him and led him away to be handed over to the procurator Pilate (Matthew 27:1–2).

Reader Two Jesus, you were wrongly accused and you did not rebel. You were mocked and flogged and you did not cry out. Help us to bear our disappointments, our weaknesses, our illnesses. Forgive us for the times we have sought retribution and blamed others for our faults.

Response: Stabat Mater

Jesus takes up the cross

Reader One The soldiers mocked Jesus, dropping to their knees before him saying: "All hail, King of the Jews." They also spat on him…. Finally, when they had finished making a fool of him, they led him off to crucifixion (Matthew 27:29–31).

Reader Two Lord, you were insulted and you did not speak out. How hard it is for us to hear criticism, to listen to others with an open mind. Help us to be more humble about our faults and to listen with true compassion. Forgive us for the times we have closed ourselves off and refused to forgive others.

Response: Stabat Mater

Simon helps to carry the cross

Reader One As they led him away, they laid hold of Simon the Cyrenean who was coming in from the fields. They put a crossbeam on Simon's shoulder for him to carry along behind Jesus (Luke 23:26).

Reader Two Lord, the weight of the cross pulled you down; our sins are borne on the wood. Help us to see the burdens some of our brothers and sisters are bearing. Give us compassion, so that we might help carry their burdens. Forgive us for the times we have failed to see their plight and neglected to reach out to them.

Response: Stabat Mater

Jesus meets the women

Reader One   A great crowd of people followed him, including women who beat their breasts and lamented over him. Jesus turned to them and said: "Daughters of Jerusalem, do not weep for me. Weep for yourselves and for your children" (Luke 23:27–28).

Reader Two   Lord, we wish to follow you. Your pain overwhelms us and we weep. Help us to look into our own hearts, to see our own faults and weaknesses, and to seek healing and forgiveness.

Response: Stabat Mater

Jesus is nailed to the cross

Reader One   When they came to Skull Place, as it was called, they crucified him there and the criminals as well, one on his right and the other on his left. Jesus cried out, "Father, forgive them; they do not know what they are doing" (Luke 23:33–34).

Reader Two   Jesus, even in pain you were able to forgive. How often have we acted without knowing what we were doing; having failed to inform ourselves before rushing to judgment. Forgive us for the times we have refused to forgive others.

Response: Stabat Mater

They divide Jesus' clothes

Reader One   They divided his garments, rolling dice for them. The soldiers also made fun of him, coming forward to offer him their sour wine and saying: "If you are the king of the Jews, save yourself." There was an inscription over his head: This is the King of the Jews. (Luke 23:34–38).

Reader Two   Lord, how often have we looked for gain in other people's pain or stood by silently while others were being wronged. Give us the strength to come to the aid of the innocent and the weak. Forgive us our weakness.

Response: Stabat Mater

Jesus dies on the cross

Reader One　　From noon onward, there was darkness over the whole land until mid-afternoon. Then Jesus cried out in a loud voice: "My God, my God, why have you forsaken me?" Once again Jesus cried out in a loud voice and then gave up his spirit (Matthew 27:45–46, 50).

Pause for silent reflection

Reader Two　　Lord, we too have forsaken you at times. We have been in darkness and we have been lost. Forgive us for the times we have lost patience with ourselves and others, for failing to trust in you.

Response: Stabat Mater

Jesus is buried

Reader One　　Joseph of Arimathea, a man who looked expectantly for the reign of God, approached Pilate with a request for Jesus' body. He took it down, wrapped it in fine linen, and laid it in a tomb hewn out of the rock, in which no one had yet been buried (Luke 23:50–53).

Reader Two　　Lord Jesus, you died for us. Like Joseph we look for the reign of God. The tomb is not the end for you and it is just the beginning for us. We have been united with you in death; we wait to be united with you in resurrection.

Response: Stabat Mater

Presider　　Let us pray: Lord we have prayerfully listened to the account of your passion and death. We know that after three days you rose from the tomb, holding out to us a new and everlasting life with you. Help us now to confess our sins and to seek forgiveness. We ask this in your holy name.

All　　Amen.

Invitation to Confession

After participants receive the sacrament, invite them to come forward to kiss or touch the cross and then to pray for a few minutes before leaving the church.

Let Peace Begin with Me

Leader's Notes

The sign of surrender in warfare has traditionally been a white flag that one side waves indicating a willingness to end hostilities. In that sense, white has become a symbolic color of peace. In this service, white ribbons would make an excellent symbol of the theme of peace. Wrap a large wreath in white ribbons, with many long ends hanging down. Staggering the length of the ends adds a beautiful effect.

If possible, hang the wreath in your worship area, or place it on a high pedestal that allows for suspension of the length of ribbons. If desired, you can give participants a lapel ribbon as they enter the church. To make these, cut a short length of ribbon and fold it in the center to form a V and attach a straight pin.

Doves are also symbols for peace. You might want to attach some doves (found in craft stores) to the ends of the ribbons.

Homily Suggestions

Peace is more of an ideal than a reality in many people's lives. This is not just because of external events and circumstances. Rather, the absence of inner peace has more to do with what is happening within us. Many are tortured by what they cannot have, and by the shortcomings of what they actually do have; perhaps the love they experience in their marriage does not seem to fulfill their deepest longings; their jobs do not measure up to the hopes they have for themselves; their homes are inadequate when compared with others; their relationships are superficial; their accomplishments are trivial. Everything seems to be insufficient. As a result many of us are always waiting, waiting for something to happen, or for somebody to come along and make things different so that we might really begin to live. Such restlessness seems to be incurable.

When something new happens in our lives, it sparks our interest, and we go out after it. But after a while it's not so new any more and we return disappointed. This going out after new things and returning disappointed tend to become a pattern in our lives. We end up being divided within ourselves. We have set our hearts on the wrong things and discovered emptiness instead of fulfillment, and eventually we find ourselves torn with regret or guilt or disappointment. But sometimes we get an insight into what is actually happening, and that we have been becoming more and more distant from our real selves, and that we need to turn to a center within us that does not depend on changing desires and circumstances.

The disciples in the boat being tossed about by the stormy sea were upset and terrified, and they were even angry with Jesus for falling asleep when they were in danger. But Jesus was surprised that they had such little trust, that they didn't feel safe, even though he was with them. It's the same with us. We are continually being tossed about by the waves of circumstances and by our own longings and desires. When things become difficult, we easily lose track of the fact that God is still close. This happens because we have such little familiarity with God's Spirit within us. But the Spirit is our baptismal gift. It's a strong center where we can anchor our little boat when it's being tossed about.

The reason for our restlessness is that we are looking for something from life that life cannot give. God has made us in such a way that our longings can never be completely satisfied in this life. St. Augustine wrote: "You have made us for yourself, O Lord, and our hearts are restless until they rest in you." God has put the Holy Spirit within us, a Spirit that will always yearn for fullness of life and love, for deep inner peace, for union with what is eternal. We must turn our restlessness into a longing for God's Spirit. That's where we can find lasting peace.

Let Peace Begin with Me

Opening Song

Opening Prayer

Presider	The Lord be with you.
All	And also with you.
Presider	Let us pray: God of compassion, our hearts cry out for peace: peace in the world, peace in our families, peace in our communities, peace in our innermost beings. We seek your peace which is beyond understanding; we seek your solace for our restless hearts. Hear our prayer and grant us our request, as we begin now in the name of the Father and of the Son and of the Holy Spirit.
All	Amen.
Presider	We come to you seeking forgiveness for our faults, our sins, and our shortcomings, and so we pray.
All	I confess to almighty God and to you my brothers and sisters that I have sinned through my own fault, in my thoughts and in my words, in what I have done and what I have failed to do, and I ask blessed Mary, ever virgin, all the angels and saints and you my brothers and sisters to pray for me to the Lord, our God.
Presider	May the God of all peace and understanding have mercy on us, listen to our requests and help us to prepare our hearts for the reception of this sacrament.

First Reading: Micah 5:1, 3–5a

Siege is laid against us; with a rod our enemies strike the ruler of Israel upon the cheek. Therefore he shall give them up until the time when she who is in labor has brought forth; then the rest of his kindred shall return to the people of Israel. And he shall stand and feed his flock in the strength of the Lord, in the majesty of the name of the Lord his God. And they shall live secure, for now he shall be great to the ends of the earth. And he shall be the one of peace.

Responsorial Psalm (Psalm 145)

Reader One	You are faithful, Lord, in all your words and holy in all your works.
All	You are faithful, Lord, in all your words and holy in all your works.
Reader Two	You, O Lord, lift up all who are falling and you raise up all who are bowed down.
All	You are faithful, Lord, in all your words and holy in all your works.
Reader One	The eyes of all look hopefully to you, and you give them their food in due season.
All	You are faithful, Lord, in all your words and holy in all your works.
Reader Two	You open your hand and satisfy the desire of every living thing.
All	You are faithful, Lord, in all your words and holy in all your works.
Reader One	You are just in all your ways and holy in all your works.
All	You are faithful, Lord, in all your words and holy in all your works.
Reader Two	You are near to all who call upon you, to all who call upon you in truth.
All	You are faithful, Lord, in all your words and holy in all your works.
Reader One	You fulfill the desire of those who fear you, you hear their cry and save them.
All	You are faithful, Lord, in all your words and holy in all your works.

Gospel Acclamation

Alleluia. Alleluia. You are the source of light and peace and goodness. May we too become peacemakers. Alleluia. Alleluia.

Gospel Reading: Mark 4:35-41

On that day, when evening had come, he said to them, "Let us go across to the other side." And leaving the crowd behind, they took him with them in the boat, just as he was. A great windstorm arose, and the waves beat into the boat, so that the boat was already being swamped. But he was in the stern, asleep on the cushion; and they woke him up and said to him, "Teacher, do you not care that we are perishing?" He woke up and rebuked the wind, and said to the sea, "Peace! Be still!" Then the wind ceased, and there was a dead calm. He said to them, "Why are you afraid? Have you still no faith?" And they were filled with great awe and said to one another, "Who then is this, that even the wind and the sea obey him?"

Homily

Meditation Song (or three minutes of silent reflection)

Examination of Conscience (based on the Prayer of St. Francis)

Reader One	Lord, make me a channel of your peace.
Reader Two	Have I tried to be a peacemaker? Have I resisted the temptation to disrupt others? Have I prayed for world peace?
All	Lord, make me a channel of your peace.
Reader One	Where there is hatred, let me sow love.
Reader Two	Have I given space to hatred in my life? Have I been unkind or even cruel in my dealings with others? Have I tried to teach my children to love and respect all others?
All	Lord, make me a channel of your peace.
Reader One	Where there is injury, pardon.
Reader Two	Have I forgiven those who have wronged me? Have I been kind to others?
All	Lord, make me a channel of your peace.
Reader One	Where there is doubt, faith.
Reader Two	Have I encouraged someone who needed support? Have I practiced my faith well? Have I been a good example of gospel living in my family and in the workplace?
All	Lord, make me a channel of your peace.
Reader One	Where there is despair, hope.
Reader Two	Have I reached out to someone who is troubled? Have I contacted someone who is lonely? Have I really listened to others who are hurting?
All	Lord, make me a channel of your peace.

Reader One	Where there is darkness, light; where there is sadness, joy.
Reader Two	Have I comforted someone who was sad? Do I bring joy and hope to those around me?
All	Lord, make me a channel of your peace.
Presider	Let us pray together now in the words of St. Francis of Assisi.
All	O Divine Master, grant that I may seek not so much to be consoled, as to console; to be understood as to understand; to be loved as to love; for it is in giving that we receive; it is in pardoning that we are pardoned, and it is in dying that we are born to eternal life. Amen.
Presider	God of peace we are here to experience your forgiveness and your love. Hear us now as we turn to you for comfort and healing. We ask this through Jesus Christ, your son, our Lord.
All	Amen.

Invitation to Confession

Following confession and quiet time for reflection, invite participants to leave the church quietly.

Come, Holy Spirit

Leader's Notes

This service, recommended for Pentecost, speaks about the gifts of the Holy Spirit. Each one of us has received many gifts, abilities, and talents. The gospel reading tells us that we are to use these talents for the benefit of others in our community.

For a visual display, cover several large boxes with bright red gift wrap. Add bows or ribbons to give them a festive look. Place them in the worship area as a visual representing giftedness. As an alternate display, place symbols of parishioners' occupations: tools, crafts, computer, finished products, to represent the many gifts the people in your parish possess.

Homily Suggestions

The church has traditionally taught that preparation for the sacrament of reconciliation consists mainly in examination of conscience, sorrow for our sins and a full confession of them. Examination of conscience has usually been understood as identifying our sins, whether of commission or omission. But that isn't everything. The Scripture readings we have just heard bring out a very important aspect of the Christian life that can't be expressed simply in terms of commandments or prohibitions. In the first reading, St. Paul teaches that everybody who has been baptized has received a gift of the Spirit for the benefit of the Christian community. The gospel reading makes it clear that God expects us to put our gifts to good use. They are like a kind of investment that God has placed with us, from which we give a return.

Our examination of ourselves therefore takes us beyond simply identifying laws of God that we have transgressed or specific obligations that we have failed to fulfill. The Word of God challenges us to look at the broader issues of responsibility and accountability in our lives. Because we have each received spiritual gifts, we are responsible for their use, and we must give an account of how well we have used them.

What are spiritual gifts for? The primary task of a Christian is the transformation of society, and that means that disciples of the Lord must have the courage to bring the values of the gospel to the world. The work of the gospel will flourish in a society where values such as freedom, respect for individual and family rights, and peace and justice, especially justice for the poor, are respected. That task is more difficult in a society where those values are not strong. So the first task of a Christian in the marketplace has to do with witness. We cannot be passive in the face of societal structures that fail to address the needs of the poor, the elderly, and other vulnerable groups.

Nor may we be passive with regard to the issue of peace. Pope John Paul has pointed out time and time again that war is no longer an adequate means for the resolution of conflicts between nations. Respect for human life at all its stages is another issue for which we are called to take a stand. This includes the church's teaching against the death penalty, because human life is God's gift, either to give or to take away.

Use of our spiritual gifts also applies to service within our own local church community, as St. Paul mentions in the first reading. Because we are a church that witnesses to the sacredness of all human life, each of us individually should be conscious of our life-giving role. Are we people who bring life to our community, or, on the contrary, do we drain life out of it? Do we see the church as merely a service organization that is supposed to provide us with a variety of services? This attitude is a far cry from that of the disciples whom Jesus gathered around him and sent out to give witness to his gospel.

Courage is a gift of the Spirit, and Christians are called to be courageous members of the human community. One of the fruits of the sacrament of reconciliation is the grace to be more faithful disciples. Let's not forget to examine ourselves about our courage in giving witness to the world and our service to our local church.

Come, Holy Spirit

Opening Song

Opening Prayer

Presider	We begin our prayer together in the name of the Father and of the Son and of the Holy Spirit.
All	Amen.
Presider	Creator God, you made us in your image and likeness, Lord have mercy.
All	Lord have mercy.
Presider	Christ Jesus, you took on our humanity and gave your life for us, Christ have mercy.
All	Christ have mercy.
Presider	You sent us your Holy Spirit to support and guide us, Lord have mercy.
All	Lord have mercy.
Presider	Hear our prayers and petitions, O God of mercy, and may your Holy Spirit give us the wisdom to recognize our sins and the courage to acknowledge them. We ask this in the name of Jesus our Lord.
All	Amen.

First Reading: 1 Corinthians 12:1, 4–11

There are varieties of gifts, but the same Spirit; and there are varieties of services, but the same Lord; and there are varieties of activities, but it is the same God who activates all of them in everyone. To each is given the manifestation of the Spirit for the common good. To one is given through the Spirit the utterance of wisdom, and to another the utterance of knowledge according to the same Spirit, to another faith by the same Spirit, to another gifts of healing by the one Spirit, to another the working of miracles, to another prophecy, to another the discernment of spirits, to another various kinds of tongues, to another the interpretation of tongues. All these are activated by one and the same Spirit, who allots to each one individually just as the Spirit chooses.

Responsorial Psalm (Psalm 139)

Reader One   O Lord, you have probed me and you know me.

All   O Lord you have probed me and you know me.

Reader Two   You know when I sit and when I stand; you understand my thoughts from afar. My journeys and my rest you scrutinize, with all my ways you are familiar.

All   O Lord you have probed me and you know me.

Reader One   Even before a word is on my tongue, behold, O Lord, you know the whole of it. Such knowledge is too wonderful for me; too lofty for me to attain.

All   O Lord you have probed me and you know me.

Reader Two   Where can I go from your spirit; from your presence where can I flee? If I go up to the heavens, you are there; if I sink to the nether world, you are present there.

All   O Lord you have probed me and you know me.

Reader One   If I take the wings of the dawn, if I settle at the farthest limits of the sea, even there your hand shall guide me, and your right hand hold me fast.

All   O Lord you have probed me and you know me.

Gospel Acclamation

Alleluia. Alleluia. You, O Holy Spirit, are the source of wisdom and understanding. Come and stay with us always. Alleluia. Alleluia.

Gospel: Matthew 25:14-29

An influential man was going on a journey, so he summoned his servants and entrusted his property to them; to one he gave five talents, to another two, to another one, to each according to his ability. Then he went away. The one who had received the five talents went off at once and traded with them, and made five more talents. In the same way, the one who had the two talents made two more talents. But the one who had received the one talent went off and dug a hole in the ground and hid his master's money. After a long time the master of those servants came and settled accounts with them. Then the one who had received the five talents came forward, bringing five more talents, saying, "Master, you handed over to me five talents; see, I have made five more talents." His master said to him, "Well done, good and trustworthy servant; you have been trustworthy in a few things, I will put you in charge of many things; enter into the joy of your master." And the one with the two talents also came forward, saying, "Master, you handed over to me two talents; see, I have made two more talents." His master said to him, "Well done, good and trustworthy servant; enter into the joy of your master." Then the one who had received the one talent also came forward, saying, "Master, I knew that you were a harsh man, reaping where you did not sow, and gathering where you did not scatter seed; so I was afraid, and I went and hid your talent in the ground. Here you have what is yours." But his master replied, "You wicked and lazy servant! You knew, did you, that I reap where I did not sow, and gather where I did not scatter? Then you ought to have invested my money, and on my return I would have received interest." He took the talent away from him, and gave it to the one with the ten talents. For to all those who have, more will be given, but from those who have nothing, even what they have will be taken away.

Homily

Meditation Song (or three minutes of silent reflection)

Examination of Conscience

Reader One	For failing to seek your wisdom.
All	Holy Spirit enlighten us.
Reader Two	For refusing to search for understanding…
All	Holy Spirit enlighten us.
Reader One	For neglecting to deepen our faith…
All	Holy Spirit enlighten us.
Reader Two	For our unwillingness to be healers to one another…
All	Holy Spirit enlighten us.
Reader One	For refusing to see the daily miracles in our lives…
All	Holy Spirit enlighten us.
Reader Two	For hiding our own talents…
All	Holy Spirit enlighten us.
Reader One	For neglecting to fully develop our gifts…
All	Holy Spirit enlighten us.
Reader Two	For our reluctance to share from our abundance…
All	Holy Spirit enlighten us.

Reader One	For failing to see the needs of the poor and the elderly…
All	Holy Spirit enlighten us.
Reader Two	For complacency in the presence of injustice…
All	Holy Spirit enlighten us.
Reader One	For losing courage when our values are challenged…
All	Holy Spirit enlighten us.
Presider	Let us pray. Merciful Lord, in baptism we received the gift of your Spirit; in the sacrament of confirmation we were strengthened in the same Spirit. Renew in us the power of your love so that we may be able to extend it to others. We ask this in your holy name.
All	Amen.

Invitation to Confession

Final Prayer and Blessing

Presider	In thanksgiving, let us raise our hearts, minds, and voices to the Holy Spirit.
All	Holy Spirit, Lord Divine, Come from heights of heaven and shine. Come with blessed radiance bright! Come, oh Father of the poor. Come, whose treasured gifts endure. Come, our heart's unfailing light. Shine on the faithful who are true And profess their faith in you. In your sevenfold gift descend! Give us virtue's sure reward. Give us your salvation, Lord. Give us joy that never ends.

—Sequence Prayer for Pentecost Sunday

Presider	Let us pray: May the Holy Spirit bless us with courage, understanding, and knowledge; may the Spirit fill us with faith, love, and joy that never ends. We ask this in Jesus' name.
All	Amen.

Closing Song

Who Is My Neighbor?

Leader's Notes

The story of the Good Samaritan is the gospel reading for this service. It is a well-known, powerful story and lends itself to dramatization. If your parish has a drama group, you might want to invite that group to act out or mime as the account is read. It can also be presented by three readers, one taking the role of the lawyer, the other the quotations from Jesus, and a third the narrations.

The examination of conscience uses the ten commandments and the great commandment of Jesus (John 13:34–35) as their basis. For a visual effect, you might want to display in your worship space large posters with these commandments written on them. Prepare small prayer cards with the "Prayer of St. Francis" (as below) on them and place them in a central place.

Lord, make me a channel of your peace.
where there is hatred, let me sow love;
where there is injury, pardon;
where there is doubt, faith;
where there is despair; hope;
where there is darkness, light;
where there is sadness, joy.

O Divine Master, grant that I may seek not so much
to be consoled as to console;
to be understood as to understand;
to be loved as to love.
For it is in giving that we receive;
it is in pardoning that we are pardoned,
and it is in dying that we are born to eternal life.
Amen.

Homily Suggestions

As we go through life, we tend to develop fixed attitudes and expectations. We come to expect certain things of familiar people, and our attitudes in certain situations become quite predictable. This is to be expected because, on the one hand, developing a pattern of fixed attitudes and expectations can help make our lives run more smoothly, and, on the other, constant adaptation to people and situations would demand more energy and be more stressful. However, there is a major drawback. Fixed attitudes and expectations tend to make us closed to what is new and unfamiliar. They leave no room for surprises. We will be inclined to reject whatever does not fit with the patterns of expectation we have established for ourselves.

Jesus encountered this problem as he tried to speak to people about the reign of God and explain its meaning to them. This was because people had fixed expectations of the messiah, and also of the reign of God. The messiah was supposed to be a military leader who would drive out the Romans, and the reign of God, when it came, would exalt the people over all the pagan nations. Such fixed expectations made people blind to the very different picture of God's reign and of the messianic mission of Jesus. But Jesus had a clever way of dealing with the blindness caused by people's fixed expectations. As a way of opening up their minds and hearts to the values of the gospel, he told stories that turned those expectations upside down.

One example is the story of the good Samaritan. People had certain definite expectations of their leaders. Priests, the teachers of the Mosaic law, and their assistants, the Levites, were expected to exemplify the justice and compassion that were the core of that law. Samaritans, on the other hand, were looked upon as worthless types, sinners who were unfaithful to the law, the kind that decent people avoided. But Jesus' parable says the opposite. It is the priests and Levites who have no compassion, while the outcast Samaritan, who breaks through ethnic and religious barriers to care for the Jew who fell among robbers, exemplifies true faithfulness to the law. With this story Jesus uncovers the blindness and prejudice of his listeners.

The priests and Levites were respectable, law-abiding citizens, the pillars of society. But many of them had become blind to the spirit of the law. While they did nothing illegal, they made sure that they took full advantage of their position to enrich themselves. Jesus criticized them for their lack of concern for widows and the poor. The Samaritans, the tax-collectors and the prostitutes, on the other hand, while breaking the letter of the law, were, according to Jesus, more faithful to its spirit.

Is it possible that we might be affected by the same blindness? Is it possible that some law-breakers may be better disciples than ourselves? Of course it is! Preparing for the sacrament of reconciliation is a good time to review our own situation. The task of uncovering blindness is a great challenge, because, if we are blind, we do not see what we need to see. It's the challenging truth in Jesus' parable that can open our eyes, if we're ready. It holds up a mirror before us, so that we may look into it and see that part of ourselves that loves to look good in front of others. That part of us seems to do all the right things, but, in reality, it's very much centered on self and personal gain, and is often blind to the requirements of compassion.

When we are willing to look in that mirror and see more clearly the truth about ourselves, then we will know that we have broken out of our fixed attitudes and expectations, that we have opened up some space for the reign of God in our lives. Our examination of conscience and our repentance will become more real.

Who Is My Neighbor?

Opening Song

Opening Prayer

Presider	As we begin our journey toward reconciliation, let us place ourselves in the presence of the Father, the Son, and the Holy Spirit.
All	Amen.
Presider	Aware of our sinfulness, we seek God's forgiveness and mercy by praying:
All	I confess to almighty God
	and to you my brothers and sisters,
	that I have sinned through my own fault,
	in my thoughts and in my words,
	in what I have done and in what I have failed to do;
	and I ask blessed Mary ever virgin,
	all the angels and saints,
	and you my brothers and sisters
	to pray for me to the Lord, our God.
Presider	Have mercy on us, O God, hear our petitions and requests, and open our hearts to your gracious Word. We ask this in the name of Jesus, our Lord.
All	Amen.

First Reading: Isaiah 35:1-6, 10

The wilderness and the dry land shall be glad, the desert shall rejoice and blossom; like the crocus it shall blossom abundantly, and rejoice with joy and singing. The glory of Lebanon shall be given to it, the majesty of Carmel and Sharon. They shall see the glory of the Lord, the majesty of our God. Strengthen the weak hands, and make firm the feeble knees. Say to those who are of a fearful heart, "Be strong, do not fear! Here is your God. He will come with vengeance, with terrible recompense. He will come and save you." Then the eyes of the blind shall be opened, and the ears of the deaf unstopped; then the lame shall leap like a deer, and the tongue of the speechless sing for joy. For waters shall break forth in the wilderness, and streams in the desert.

And the ransomed of the Lord shall return, and come to Zion with singing; everlasting joy shall be upon their heads; they shall obtain joy and gladness, and sorrow and sighing shall flee away.

Responsorial Psalm (Psalm 148)

Right Side	We praise you, Lord, from the heavens, we praise you from the heights;
Left Side	All your angels praise you, all your heavenly hosts.
Right Side	We praise you with the sun and moon; we praise you with all your shining stars.
Left Side	We praise your name, for your name alone is exalted.
Right Side	Your majesty is above earth and heaven, and you have lifted up your people.
Left Side	May all your faithful ones praise you and may they bless your holy name.
All	Amen.

Gospel Acclamation

Alleluia. Alleluia. We are your faithful people, O God; help us to love and care for our neighbors. Alleluia. Alleluia.

Gospel: Luke 10:25-37

Just then a lawyer stood up to test Jesus. "Teacher," he said, "what must I do to inherit eternal life?" Jesus said to him, "What is written in the law? What do you read there?" He answered, "You shall love the Lord your God with all your heart, and with all your soul, and with all your strength, and with all your mind; and your neighbor as yourself." And he said to him, "You have given the right answer; do this, and you will live." But wanting to justify himself, he asked Jesus, "And who is my neighbor?" Jesus replied, "A man was going down from Jerusalem to Jericho, and fell into the hands of robbers, who stripped him, beat him, and went away, leaving him half dead. Now by chance a priest was going down that road; and when he saw him, he passed by on the other side. So likewise a Levite, when he came to the place and saw him, passed by on the other side. But a Samaritan while traveling came near him; and when he saw him, he was moved with pity.

He went to him and bandaged his wounds and then took him to an inn and cared for him. The next day he paid the innkeeper, and said, "Take care of him; and when I come back, I will repay you whatever more you spend." Which of these three, do you think, was a neighbor to the man who fell into the hands of the robbers?" He said, "The one who showed him mercy." Jesus said to him, "Go and do likewise."

Homily

Meditation Song (or three minutes of silent reflection)

Examination of Conscience

Reader One	You shall Love the Lord, your God... Have I neglected opportunities in my life for prayer and reflection? Have I missed Mass on Sundays without sufficient reason?
All	Lord, we seek forgiveness.
Reader Two	You shall not take the name of the Lord, your God in vain... Have I been careless with my words? Have I been disrespectful of others and unduly argumentative?
All	Lord, we seek forgiveness
Reader One	Honor your father and mother... Have I been respectful of my parents? Have I been respectful of older people? Have I tried to help those who needed my help?
All	Lord, we seek forgiveness.
Reader Two	You shall not commit adultery; you shall not steal; you shall not covet... Have I been unfaithful to my spouse? Have I been envious of the good fortune of others? Have I been jealous or desired another's belongings? Have I sinned against these commandments in other ways?
All	Lord, we seek forgiveness.
Reader One	You shall love your neighbor as yourself... Have I been aware of the needs of my neighbor? Have I been willing to give to those in need? Have I recognized those of different cultures and races as my neighbor? Have I been blind to my own faults?

All	Lord, we seek forgiveness.
Presider	Let us pray: Lord, in the story of the good Samaritan you show us that all people are our neighbors, that all are our brothers and sisters. Help us to be aware of the needs of others, and strengthen our desire to reach out to all those in need. We ask this through Christ, our Lord.
All	Amen.
Reader One	As we prepare to confess our sins, let us pray in the words that Jesus taught us:
All	Our Father, who art in heaven…

Invitation to Confession

After they have received the sacrament, invite participants to take one of the prayer cards and silently reflect on it as their penance.

Father, I Have Sinned

Leader's Notes

In this service the well-known gospel of the prodigal son is the focal point. This gospel is very effective when read by three readers: the part of the Son, the part of the Father, and a narrator. As the gospel is read, props can be brought forward for visual effect. (Money bags, straw, a corn stalk, etc). At the conclusion of the reading, a robe, a pair of sandals, and a ring can be brought to the worship area and placed on a table.

Following this service, you could provide refreshments for a celebration of forgiveness—as in the gospel story.

Homily Suggestions

The story of the prodigal son is perhaps the most well-known of all the stories that Jesus told. It's a universal story, for all times and cultures. After 2000 years, it hasn't lost any of its power. The reason is that it speaks to a very universal human experience, the relationship between parents and their children, the rebellion of young people against the authority of their parents, and the reconciliation that is needed within all families from time to time.

What this story really is about, of course, is the relationship between God and ourselves. Let's look at the details for a moment. The younger son said to his father, "Give me my share of the inheritance." He couldn't wait for his father to die off. He was anxious to get away from home, where he could be totally free from any parental supervision. There would be money in his pocket and a good time to be had without anybody looking over his shoulder. He was confident that everything would be fine if he could just get away from home. His father didn't complain, he just did what his son asked of him. I'm sure the people listening to the story must have said to themselves, "What a foolish old man!"

Anyway, his son went off to a foreign country and had a good time with plenty of fair-weather friends, as long as his money lasted. But when the famine came, they abandoned him, and he was forced to take a job feeding pigs. We must bear in mind that Jews are forbidden to have anything to do with pigs; they associated them with demons. Jesus is telling us just how low his selfishness and self-indulgence had brought the prodigal son; he had degraded himself to the lowest level. The good times had not brought him any real happiness.

Finally we're told, he came to his senses. He began to see the reality of his situation. He had been blind to his father's love and he had been looking for happiness in the wrong places. He decided to return to his father's house. His father had never forgotten him. He had never stopped loving him, in spite of what he had done. He went out scanning the horizon for him every day, until finally he saw him on the road. We're told that he ran out to meet him, threw his arms around his neck and kissed him.

There's something else we might take note of here. Older men in Jewish society were patriarchal figures, they moved about slowly with great dignity. They didn't run; they waited for people to come to them. Again we can imagine the listening people saying to themselves, "What a silly old man, making a fool of himself running out to welcome back such a son." But the father makes no complaint. There's no punishment, no reminder of past warnings, no, "I told you so." There's only joy and celebration.

And that's the point of the whole story. The one who loves us to the point of foolishness is none other than God our Father. We are all God's lost children, being welcomed back home. This is a story about ourselves and our sinful ways, our failure to love and forgive. It's about our love of money and possessions and our blindness to what's really important. Above all it's about God our Father who is scanning the horizon every day with great love to see if we will finally come to our senses and return home.

Father, I Have Sinned

Opening Song

Opening Prayer

Presider	We are God's children who sometimes lose our way, but we are always welcomed back with great joy by our heavenly father. No matter how far we have strayed, no matter how lost we are, we can pray confidently in the name of the Father and of the Son and of the Holy Spirit.
All	Amen.
Presider	The Lord be with you.
All	And also with you.
Presider	Let us pray: God of mercy, our journey leads us back to you. We come from you and we seek to be welcomed back into your arms. We stray from you at times and we ask your help to find our way back. Forgive us so that we may once again dwell with you. Lord, we have sinned against you, Lord have mercy…
All	Lord have mercy.
Presider	Christ, we return to you with contrite hearts, Christ have mercy…
All	Christ have mercy.
Presider	Lord, open your arms to receive us back, Lord have mercy…
All	Lord have mercy.
Presider	May God our Father help us to acknowledge our sins and transgressions with contrite and humble hearts.
All	Amen.

First Reading: Sirach 17:17-24

Lord God, you have appointed a ruler for every nation, but Israel is your own portion. All the works of your chosen people are as clear as the sun before you, and your eyes are ever upon their ways. Their iniquities are not hidden from you, and all their sins are before you. Yet to those who repent you grant a return, and you encourage those who are losing hope.

Responsorial Psalm (Psalm 103)

Reader One	Bless the Lord, O my soul!
All	I bless you, O Lord, with all my soul.
Reader Two	All my being, blesses your holy name.
All	I bless you, O Lord, with all my soul.
Reader One	I will never forget all your blessings.
All	I bless you, O Lord, with all my soul.
Reader Two	You pardon all my iniquities; you heal all my ills.
All	I bless you, O Lord, with all my soul.
Reader One	Merciful and gracious are you, Lord, slow to anger and abounding in kindness.
All	I bless you, O Lord, with all my soul.
Reader Two	As parents have compassion on their children; so you, Lord, have compassion on those who fear you.
All	I bless you, O Lord, with all my soul.

Gospel Acclamation

Alleluia. Alleluia. We have turned our hearts away from you, O God. You lead us back and forgive our sins. Alleluia. Alleluia.

Gospel Reading: Luke 15:11-24

Then Jesus said, "There was a man who had two sons. The younger of them said to his father, 'Father, give me the share of the property that will belong to me.' So he divided his property between them. A few days later the younger son gathered all he had and traveled to a distant country, and there he squandered his property in dissolute living. When he had spent everything, a severe famine took place throughout that country, and he began to be in need. So he went and hired himself out to one of the citizens of that country, who sent him to his fields to feed the pigs. He would gladly have filled himself with the pods that the pigs were eating; but no one gave him anything. When he came to himself he said, 'How many of my father's hired hands have bread enough and to spare, but here I am dying of hunger! I will get up and go to my father, and I will say to him, "Father, I have sinned against heaven and before you; I am no longer worthy to be called your son; treat me like one of your hired hands."' So he set off and went to his father. But while he was still far off, his father saw him and was filled with compassion; he ran and put his arms around him and kissed him. Then the son said to him, 'Father, I have sinned against heaven and before you; I am no longer worthy to be called your son.' But the father said to his slaves, 'Quickly, bring out a robe —the best one—and put it on him; put a ring on his finger and sandals on his feet. And get the fatted calf and kill it, and let us eat and celebrate; for this son of mine was dead and is alive again; he was lost and is found!' And they began to celebrate."

Homily

Meditation Song (or three minutes of silent reflection)

Examination of Conscience

Reader One	For our insensitivity…
All	Forgive us, Lord.
Reader Two	For our thoughtlessness…
All	Forgive us, Lord.
Reader One	For our greediness…
All	Forgive us, Lord.
Reader Two	For our lack of understanding…
All	Forgive us, Lord.
Reader One	For our refusal to help…
All	Forgive us, Lord.
Reader Two	For our failure to give comfort…
All	Forgive us, Lord.
Reader One	For our lack of gratitude…
All	Forgive us, Lord.
Reader Two	For our judgmental attitude…
All	Forgive us, Lord.
Reader One	For our impatience…
All	Forgive us, Lord.
Reader Two	For our greed…
All	Forgive us, Lord.
Reader One	For our jealousy…

All	Forgive us, Lord.
Reader Two	For all our transgressions…
All	Forgive us, Lord.
Presider	Let us pray: Merciful God, we admit that we too have sinned against you and like the son who was lost, we ask for your forgiveness. Welcome us back, greet us with open arms, and grant us your mercy and your love. We ask this in the name of Jesus our brother.
All	Amen.

Invitation to Confession

Final Prayer and Dismissal

Presider	God our loving Father has welcomed us back and received us with joy; in celebration, let us extend a sign of peace and joy to one another.

Exchange a sign of peace, for example: "May the peace of our forgiving God be with you."

Presider	Let us pray: Lord you have renewed in us your spirit; may we share your gifts of joy and hope with everyone we meet. We ask these things in the name of the Father and of the Son and of the Holy Spirit.
All	Amen.

Closing Song

Forgive Us, Lord

Leader's Notes

This service is very effective as a mime. Mimers need not be experienced actors, but all should have the traditional white face (makeup available in craft stores) and wear simple black clothes to focus attention on the action. The mime should be done at the time of the gospel. Once the group leaves the altar area (as below), the gospel should be proclaimed.

Directions for the Mime

• A number of people enter the worship area in groups of two or three, entering from different directions; they carry colorful balls in their hands. As they meet, they greet each other and some begin throwing balls to one another. Some are conversing, others sharing mementos or photographs with one another. The scene should convey people getting along and enjoying one another.

• A person enters from the side, wearing a bright piece of clothing, such as a scarf. This person is looking unfriendly, does not greet anyone, but just barges into the middle of the group, nudging others out of the way. He or she does not have a ball and after a while, grabs one. This person then moves to the outside, turning his back to the happy group. He looks at the ball he has taken and having no one to play with, abandons it. The others continue their activity, but are aware of the "outcast" and eventually someone points to that person.

• Most of the group ignores the outsider, but one person goes over and touches him or her on the shoulder. He looks around, surprised, and after some persuasion agrees to join the rest of the people. After some initial reluctance, they reach out their hands to the outsider who with a small bow also reaches out to them. Finally, someone gives him a ball and they all start playing together. The lonely one smiles and the group leaves together.

Appropriate background music enhances this mime.

Homily Suggestions

Both forgiveness and reconciliation seem easy when we watch them being acted out in a mime, but all of us know that this is not actually the case. Whether we've offended someone, or someone has hurt us, it often takes some time to come to reconciliation—sometimes a long time. Some people carry the burden of unreconciled feelings for years, others never reconcile at all. In fact, eight stages can be identified in the process of turning back to someone in these situations. They are: anger, denial, isolation, helplessness, self-pity, doubt, initiative, and reconciliation. Let's try and relate these stages to the mime we just watched.

The first stage is anger. What did people feel when the newcomer barged into the group, and then proceeded to take one of their balls? Anger. We've all had that feeling when someone doesn't treat us with respect or consideration.

Anger easily leads to denial, denial that we are in any way responsible for what has happened. But why did this person barge into the group and act in an aggressive manner? The most likely reason is that he or she felt excluded. So we need to look at our denials. When we stop denying, we will often have to admit that we ourselves are not completely blameless.

Then there is isolation. Our anger and denial cause us to withdraw emotionally from the person who has offended us. We don't allow ourselves to ask about what he or she has been feeling. We close the door of our heart to that person.

This leads to helplessness. The painful, unreconciled situation remains there between us, but we have isolated ourselves with our anger and our denial, and we therefore feel helpless to do anything about it.

Helplessness can easily lead us to feel sorry for ourselves—to wallow in self-pity. We tell ourselves that we are the offended party, we are not guilty. We did not take any aggressive action. It is up to the other person to step forward now and do something about it.

If we are honest with ourselves, some self-doubt may enter in after a while. When we reflect on the background to what has happened, we begin to realize that we are not entirely guiltless. Perhaps the aggressive person had reason to be angry because he or she had been ignored or even ridiculed by our group for some time. That does not excuse that person's behavior, but now we no longer feel good about doing nothing.

This is where we come to the "initiative" stage. You noticed that someone in the group took the initiative and eventually reached out and touched the outsider on the shoulder. It was a short journey after that to full reconciliation and incorporation of that person into the group.

The important thing to remember is that all of us cause hurt sometimes. All of us therefore need to ask for forgiveness, and all of us need to forgive even those who don't ask for it. When we can do this, we will be inwardly free and unburdened, and we'll be able to praise God for whatever happens. That's why Jesus included the blessing of forgiving and being forgiven in his own special prayer that he taught his disciples.

Forgive Us, Lord

Opening Song

Opening Prayer

Presider	We begin our prayer together in the name of the Father and of the Son and of the Holy Spirit.
All	Amen.
Presider	The Lord be with you.
All	And also with you.
Presider	Loving God, you have said: "If my people, upon whom my name has been pronounced, humble themselves and pray, and seek my presence and turn from their evil ways, I will hear them from heaven and pardon their sins" (2 Chronicles 7:14). We are your people; we seek your presence and we want to turn from our sins. Hear our prayer, forgive us, and lead us back to you. We ask this in the name of Jesus, our Lord.
All	Amen.
Presider	Lord, we your people, seek your presence, Lord have mercy…
All	Lord have mercy.
Presider	Christ, we your people seek your forgiveness, Christ have mercy…
All	Christ have mercy.
Presider	Lord, we your people seek your counsel, Lord have mercy…
All	Lord have mercy.
Presider	May the Lord be with us, to open our eyes to the wrong we have done, so that we may truly be able to seek pardon and find peace.
All	Amen.

Mime (see directions on page 71)

Gospel Acclamation

Alleluia. Alleluia. You are the great one, the God of our ancestors and the God of our children. Forgive our sins, O God, our God. Alleluia. Alleluia.

Gospel Mime Reading: Matthew 6:9-15

Jesus said to his disciples, "Pray then in this way: Our Father in heaven, hallowed be your name. Your kingdom come. Your will be done, on earth as it is in heaven. Give us this day our daily bread. And forgive us our debts, as we also have forgiven our debtors. And do not bring us to the time of trial, but rescue us from the evil one. For if you forgive others their trespasses, your heavenly Father will also forgive you; but if you do not forgive others, neither will your Father forgive your trespasses."

Homily

Meditation Song (or three minutes of silent reflection)

Examination of Conscience

Reader One   Father, hallowed be your name, your kingdom come (Luke 11:2).

Reader Two   Have we respected God's name? Have we tried to use our gifts and talents to help others and thus bring about God's Kingdom? Have we tried to be peacemakers in our homes, workplaces, and with our friends?

All   Forgive us, Lord.

Reader One   Father, forgive them; they do not know what they are doing (Luke 23:34).

Reader Two   Have we been insensitive to others? Have we excluded someone from our friendship? Have we tried to reach out to a lonely person?

All   Forgive us, Lord.

Reader One   Forgive us our sins for we too forgive all who do us wrong (Luke 11:4).

Reader Two   Have we forgiven those who offended us? Have we tried to reach out to those who disagree with us? Do we listen with compassion to our spouse, our children, our co-workers?

All   Forgive us, Lord.

Reader One   Ask and you shall receive; seek and you shall find; knock and it shall be opened to you (Luke 11:9).

Reader Two   Have we been willing to ask others for help? Have we been able to trust in prayer? Have we tried to be patient? Have we sought advice and counsel in difficult situations?

All	Forgive us, Lord.
Reader One	Subject us not to the trial but deliver us from the evil one (Matthew 6:13).
Reader Two	Have we judged or accused others falsely? Have we passed along gossip or broken confidences? Have we tried to be tolerant of others?
All	Forgive us, Lord.
Presider	As a sign of our willingness to change, let us pray together the prayer Jesus taught us.
All	Our Father, who art in heaven…

Invitation to Confession

Final Prayer and Blessing

Presider	Let us pray: Lord, you know our sins and yet have called us back to you. You have blessed us with forgiveness. We ask your blessing as well on all those we have wronged. Strengthen us to stay ever near you; protect our families and friends and keep all in your loving care. We ask this, through Christ our Lord.
All	Amen.
Presider	Having experienced God's peace, let us now exchange a sign of peace.

Exchange a sign of peace, for example: "May Christ's peace be within you."

Presider	May the Lord continue to comfort us and give us peace, in the name of the Father and of the Son and of the Holy Spirit.
All	Amen.

Closing Song